Dedicated to Holly

# This is a book about the platypus...

# A rare and unique creature!

# I'd like to tell you all about...

# The platypuses amazing features!

# The platypus has a BILL - LIKE A DUCK...

# Yet it doesn't make the sound QUACK QUACK...

# And the platypus has webbed feet...

# On the front and the back!

# The platypus has a tail like a beaver...

# Which helps it move quickly through water.

# Their bill keeps the water out...

# So they can continue hunting for longer.

# The male platypus has a stinger...

# Near the back of his leg in a gland...

# The stinger has poison in it...

# Which is dangerous to predators and man.

# And now it's time to JUMP JUMP JUMP...

# And SNUFFLE, SNUFFLE, SNUFFLE LIKE A PLATYPUS!

# A baby platypus is called a PUGGLE...

# A baby echidna is a PUGGLE too!

# A newborn platypus puggle is the size of a paper clip...

# While their weight is similar to that of a kiwi fruit.

# Platypuses live in Australia...

# In the rivers and streams of Tasmania and Queensland...

# Since they don't have teeth...

# They always mush up the food they catch again and again.

# And now it's time to JUMP JUMP JUMP...

# And SNUFFLE, SNUFFLE, SNUFFLE
# LIKE A PLATYPUS!

# A group of platypuses are called a PADDLE...

# The platypus is a mammal, it's true...

# Even though the mother platypus lays eggs.

# A puggle hatches in ten days, it's true.

# Platypuses can be shy...

# So, if you see a platypus near you...

# Then you know you're in Australia!

# And you might want to...

# JUMP JUMP JUMP
## and SNUFFLE, SNUFFLE, SNUFFLE,
## LIKE A PLATYPUS!

# WE

# PLATYPUS

# SNUFFLES!

## Jump Series:

Jump Like a Caribou!
Jump Like a Kangaroo!
Jump at the Zoo!
Jump and Say P.U.!
Jump and Say Boo!
Jump and Say Valentine's Day Is
For Kids Too!
Jump and Look For a Clue!
Jump and Say Happy Birthday to You!
Jump For Everything Blue!
Jump, Hop and Say Happy Easter To You!
Jump and Say Cock-A-Doodle-Do!
Jump and Sing Da-Do-Do-Do!
Jump and Ask Who? Who?
Jump and Squawk Like a Cockatoo!
Jump and Ask Is It You or Ewe?
Jump and Say There's an Ewww in My Stew!
Jump and Say Merry Christmas To You!
Jump and Cheer Happy New Year!
Jump and Say There's a Moo-Moo in a Tutu!
Jump and Say There's a Hare in My Hair!
Jump and Say My Aunt Ate An Ant!
Jump and Say There's An Aardvark
In The Amusement Park!

Jump and Roar For The Dinosaurs!
Jump and Buzz Like A Bee!
Jump and Flutter Like A Butterfly!
Jump and Pop Like Popcorn!
Jump and Ribbit Like A Frog!
Jump and Snore Like A Koala!

Clap For Series
Clap for 1!
Clap for 2!
Clap for 3!
Clap for 4!
Clap for 5!
Clap for 6!
Clap for 7!
Clap for 8!
Clap for 9!
Clap for 10!

The Cat Who Said Hello
The Three Boulders
Billy Shakespeare/Billie Shakespeare
Learn To Draw With Symmetry
ABC More Learn to Draw With Symmetry

Non-Fiction
103 Fundraising Ideas For Parent Volunteers With
Schools and Teams

www.ingramcontent.com/pod-product-compliance
Lightning Source LLC
Chambersburg PA
CBHW051249120626
46547CB00014B/1862